Tom Frazer is a barrister practising from Selborne Chambers in all areas of property and commercial chancery law. He is based in London, but frequently acts in proceedings across the breadth of England and Wales. Tom is also called to the Bar in the British Virgin Islands, acting as a consultant to, and appearing on behalf of, law firms within that jurisdiction. Tom has a first-class degree in ancient history from the University of Bristol and studied for his Graduate Diploma in Law at City University London. He is qualified to accept direct access work.

A Practical Guide to Visual Intrusion and the Tort of Nuisance

A Practical Guide to Visual Intrusion and the Tort of Nuisance

Tom Frazer

Barrister, Selborne Chambers

Middle Temple

Law Brief Publishing

Published 2024 by Law Brief Publishing, an imprint of Law Brief Publishing Ltd
30 The Parks
Minehead
Somerset
TA24 8BT

www.lawbriefpublishing.com

Paperback: 978-1-916698-36-9

PREFACE

At the start of 2023, the Supreme Court handed down its judgment in the case of *Fearn & Ors v Board of Trustees of the Tate Gallery* [2024] AC 1. Overturning the judgment of the Court of Appeal, Lord Leggatt, giving the judgment of the majority, confirmed that 'visual intrusion' could, conceptually, give rise to liability in the tort of nuisance. The Supreme Court has also provided a restatement of several principles guiding liability in nuisance more generally, in particular on the test of 'common and ordinary use' and the role of reasonableness in the tort.

The extent to which the species of nuisance now known as visual intrusion proves to be a rich seam for future litigation remains to be seen. The facts of *Fearn* itself are very unlikely to reoccur. Nevertheless, it is appropriate at this early juncture to examine in some detail the nature of the judgment given by the Supreme Court, to understand what exactly is meant by 'visual intrusion' and the sort of cases that may fall under its heading, alongside examining how it is located within the wider tort of nuisance.

The law in this text is believed by the author to be correct and up to date as of 1 May 2024.

With thanks to Tim Kevan, Garry Wright and Law Brief Publishing, as well as the clerking and marketing teams at Selborne Chambers.

Tom Frazer
May 2024

CONTENTS

INTRODUCTION

'VISUAL INTRUSION' AND THE CASE OF *FEARN*

Fearn v Board of Trustees of the Tate Gallery

A discussion of visual intrusion and the tort of nuisance can only begin in one place: the Blavatnik Building at the Tate Modern art gallery in London. This building, and in particular the viewing gallery on its top floor, was at the centre of the dispute in *Fearn & Ors v Board of Trustees of the Tate Gallery*.[1] The claim was brought by several residents in the nearby Neo Bankside residential development, which consisted of a block of flats with floor to ceiling glass windows. Visitors to the Tate had '*a clear and uninterrupted view of how the claimants seek to conduct their lives,*'[2] and utilised this view to the full: '*some look, some peer, some photograph, some wave. Occasionally binoculars are used. Many photographs showing the interiors of the flats have been posted on social media.*'[3]

It is perhaps little surprise that the occupiers of those flats sought to put a stop to this intrusion. They brought a claim against the Tate, relying, amongst other grounds, on the cause of action of nuisance. At

1 *Fearn & Ors v Board of Trustees of the Tate Gallery* [2024] AC 1 (SC)

2 *Fearn & Ors v Board of Trustees of the Tate Gallery* [2024] AC 1 (SC) [2]

3 *Fearn & Ors v Board of Trustees of the Tate Gallery* [2024] AC 1 (SC) [5]

first instance,[4] Mann J dismissed the claim. In doing so, he recognised the potential for intrusive viewing to form the basis of a cause of action in nuisance, but nevertheless, having applied what he considered to be the correct test of 'reasonable user', he found that Tate's use of the viewing gallery was not tortious. The claimants appealed the first instance decision, and the matter was heard by the Court of Appeal,[5] with a bench consisting of Sir Terence Etherton MR, Lewison LJ and Rose LJ. The appeal was dismissed, the court unanimously determining that "overlooking" could not give rise to a cause of action in nuisance.

The claimants appealed again to the Supreme Court. By a majority of three (Lord Leggatt, Lord Reed PSC and Lord Lloyd-Jones) to two (Lord Sales and Lord Kitchin), the Court of Appeal's decision was overturned. In the lead judgment, Lord Leggatt affirmed that visual intrusion could give rise to a cause of action in nuisance, and that the invitation by the Tate of hundreds of thousands of members of the public onto its viewing platform constituted a tortious interference with the claimants' use of their land.

The circumstances of *Fearn* are somewhat unique. Nevertheless, Lord Leggatt's judgment has opened the door to visual intrusion as a novel species (in a loose sense) of nuisance, in particular of nuisance for the interference with the use and value of land. *Fearn*'s greatest contribution to the law of nuisance may well prove to be its evaluation and restatement of the test for liability under this cause of action

---

4 *Fearn & Ors v Board of Trustees of the Tate Gallery* [2019] Ch. 369 (HC)

5 *Fearn & Ors v Board of Trustees of the Tate Gallery* [2020] Ch. 621 (CA)

which, at least in the eyes of the dissenting minority, is a departure from the prior position.

A consideration of visual intrusion is therefore indivisible from a discussion of *Fearn*, and this work will seek to locate the place of both in the wider context of the tort of nuisance. Further, as noted by Lord Carnwath in the Supreme Court case of *Lawrence v Fen Tigers Ltd*,[6] prior to that case nuisance, in particular nuisance for interference with the use of land, was an area that had received little attention at the highest level.[7] A review of the principles arising out of both *Lawrence* and *Fearn* is therefore useful, and the introduction of visual intrusion to the tort provides the opportunity to do so.

'Visual Intrusion'

It is first necessary to consider exactly what is meant by the term 'visual intrusion.' It is an expression used only once in the judgment of Mann J at first instance in *Fearn*[8] and not at all by the Court of Appeal. In the Supreme Court, by contrast, it is the chosen description for the offending interference that gave rise to liability, both conceptually and on the facts of the case,[9] and is likely to be the name by which this particular species of nuisance will be referred to going forward. A definition of sorts is given by Lord Leggatt:

6 *Lawrence v Fen Tigers Ltd* [2014] AC 822

7 *Lawrence v Fen Tigers Ltd* [2014] AC 822 at [175]

8 *Fearn & Ors v Board of Trustees of the Tate Gallery* [2019] Ch. 369 (HC) at [17]

9 *Fearn & Ors v Board of Trustees of the Tate Gallery* [2024] AC 1 (SC) at [104]

> "*In this case we are concerned, not with a sight to which an occupier of land is subjected when looking out, but with the interference caused by people constantly looking in*"[10]

In order words, the act complained of is not an intrusion on the vision of the complainant, but rather the interference with the complainant's use of their property by the intrusive vision of another. The distinction is an important one, as it separates what may fall within the scope of 'visual intrusion' from those cases, such as the right to light cases or, as in *Hunter v Canary Wharf Ltd*[11], interference with the claimant's television arial, in which conceptual liability in nuisance has long been established.

One further important point in respect of the definition is that, in this context, <u>it is not synonymous with 'overlooking'</u>. The phrase 'overlooking' received extensive consideration in Lord Leggatt's judgment, and indeed was the nomenclature for the prospective cause of action rejected by the Court of Appeal. The distinction, as will be examined in Chapter Three, is an important one: whilst 'visual intrusion' is capable of amounting to a tort, 'mere overlooking' is not.

It is the aim of this work to bring some clarity to the phrase 'visual intrusion', by placing Lord Leggatt's discussion of the term in the context of the wider cause of action of nuisance. In **Chapter One**, the nature and loose categorisation of nuisance will be looked at, with visual intrusion located within that structure, before some of the essential elements of the cause of action are considered. **Chapter Two** will consider in more detail Lord Leggatt's lead judgment in the Supreme Court in *Fearn* on the question of what constitutes a

---

10 *Fearn & Ors v Board of Trustees of the Tate Gallery* [2024] AC 1 (SC) at [16]

11 *Hunter v Canary Wharf Ltd* [1997] AC 655

'substantial interference', and in particular its relationship to the principle of reasonableness. In **Chapter Three** examples of the type of conduct that may amount to visual intrusion, both as given in *Fearn* and arising from other case law, will be explored. **Chapter Four** will look at some defences that may be available to visual intrusion claims, as well as principles and arguments that have been held not to amount to defences. **Chapter Five** will consider the remedies that may be available in a visual intrusion claim, focussing on injunctive relief, damages in lieu of an injunction, and damages generally.

CHAPTER ONE

VISUAL INTRUSION IN THE CONTEXT OF NUISANCE

Locating 'Visual Intrusion' in Nuisance

There is no tort of visual intrusion. The tort, the cause of action, is nuisance; visual intrusion is simply a convenient descriptor for a species of interference with land that may give rise to an actionable nuisance.

Nuisance is a tort of considerable ambit, without any conceptual or *a priori* limit as to what it is constituted by.[1] The categories of nuisance, famously, are not closed.[2] It is protean in nature,[3] and whilst in *Hunter v Canary Wharf Ltd* Lord Hope noted its difficulty to define,[4] this was attempted by Lord Neuberger in *Lawrence v Fen Tigers*:[5]

> *"A nuisance can be defined, albeit in general terms, as an action (or sometimes a failure to act) on the part of a*

---

1 *Fearn & Ors v Board of Trustees of the Tate Gallery* [2024] AC 1 (SC) at [12]

2 *Donoghue v Stevenson* [1932] AC 562, 619

3 *Sedleigh-Denfield v O'Calaghan* [1940] AC 880, 903; *Hunter v Canary Wharf Ltd* [1997] AC 655, 723B

4 *Hunter v Canary Wharf Ltd* [1997] AC 655, 723B

5 *Lawrence v Fen Tigers Ltd* [2014] AC 822 at [3]

> *defendant, which is not otherwise authorised, and which causes an interference with the claimant's reasonable enjoyment of his land, or to use a slightly different formulation, which unduly interferes with the claimant's enjoyment of his land."*

Following the Supreme Court in *Fearn*, as discussed in Chapter Two, care must be taken in respect of the relevance of reasonableness in an assessment of liability.

Whether or not the scope of the tort was wide enough to encompass claims for visual intrusion was an issue throughout the *Fearn* proceedings. Mann J in the High Court, addressing the question in terms of whether invasion of privacy could constitute a nuisance, found that it could;[6] the Court of Appeal, considering whether 'overlooking' was a nuisance, found that it was not.[7] The Supreme Court, distinguishing visual intrusion from 'overlooking' (a distinction that is examined in the next chapter), has definitively settled this question. Reviewing authorities, both in this jurisdiction and perhaps more persuasively in other common law jurisdictions, Lord Leggatt, giving the judgment of the majority, held as follows:

> *"I conclude that, as well as being contrary to principle, the notion that visual intrusion cannot constitute a nuisance is not supported by precedent and indeed that such direct*

6 *Fearn & Ors v Board of Trustees of the Tate Gallery* [2019] Ch. 369 (HC) at [164]-[179]

7 *Fearn & Ors v Board of Trustees of the Tate Gallery* [2020] Ch. 621 (CA) at [50]-[84]

> *authority as there is positively supports the opposite conclusion."* [8]

Visual intrusion, therefore, can now be considered a species of nuisance; however, locating its relation to the wider tort does not end there. In *Hunter v Canary Wharf Ltd*, Lord Lloyd divided private nuisance into three classes[9] (a categorisation that was seemingly adopted by Lord Hope[10]):

> *"Private nuisances are of three kinds: they are (1) nuisance by encroachment on a neighbour's land; (2) nuisance by direct physical injury to a neighbour's land; and (3) nuisance by interference with a neighbour's quiet enjoyment of his land".*

The Court of Appeal has, more recently, qualified these categories '*as merely examples of a violation of property rights*'[11], stressing the difficulty with any rigid categorisation.[12] Nevertheless, whilst bearing in mind the absence of any formality in the distinction and recognising the flexible nature of the tort as a whole, it is likely to remain useful to practitioners and courts to analyse nuisance in accordance with Lord Lloyd's three classes.

Where, then, does visual intrusion stand in relation to other species of nuisance? It does not, as with examples such as interference with an easement or *Rylands v Fletcher* cases, have sufficiently clearly defined

---

8 *Fearn & Ors v Board of Trustees of the Tate Gallery* [2024] AC 1 (SC) at [104]

9 *Hunter v Canary Wharf Ltd* [1997] AC 655, 695B-C

10 *Hunter v Canary Wharf Ltd* [1997] AC 655, 724F

11 *Williams v Network Rail Infrastructure Ltd* [2019] QB 601 at [41]

12 *Williams v Network Rail Infrastructure Ltd* [2019] QB 601 at [41]

edges so as almost to appear as a cause of action in and of itself. Nor is it, like 'Japanese knotweed' or 'tree-root' cases, so tightly aligned to a particular basis in fact as to be capable of ring-fencing with any confidence. It is closer in nature to the more amorphous categories of 'noise', 'smells' etc which, whilst providing a broadly coherent heading, give plenty of scope for an indefinable multitude of factual bases. Nevertheless, 'visual intrusion' is very likely to fall within the third of Lord Lloyd's classes, namely nuisance by interference with the use and quiet enjoyment of land. Indeed, this is how it has been treated *obiter* in the Supreme Case of *Jalla v Shell International Trading*[13] (which wrongly applied the term 'overlooked' to describe the tortious act).

Essential elements of the cause of action

It is beyond the scope of this work to examine in any detail the elements of the cause of action of nuisance by interference with use of land that are common to all such cases, and the reader is referred to more general texts on the law of nuisance for the same. Nevertheless, a claimant seeking to establish liability for visual intrusion will have to satisfy those elements. It is therefore appropriate to address, in summary, some matters that should be born in mind.

---

13 *Jalla v Shell International Trading* [2023] UKSC 16 at [3]

Nuisance is a tort to land

Private nuisance is a tort to land.[14] Its subject matter is the wrongful interference with the claimant's enjoyments of rights over land. In Lord Leggatt's identification of the core principles of nuisance in *Fearn*, reflecting its central importance to the tort, this principle was listed first.[15] As identified by Lord Leggatt:

> *"It follows from the nature of the tort of private nuisance that the harm from which the law protects a claimant is diminution in the utility and amenity value of the claimant's land, and not personal discomfort to the persons who are occupying it."* [16]

This echoes a similar statement in *Hunter*, in which Lord Hope identified the true measure of liability as '*the extent to which the nuisance has impeded the comfortable enjoyment of the plaintiff's property.*'[17]

Consequently, as Lord Leggatt states, the personal discomfort of a person occupying land caused by visual intrusion does not give rise to liability in nuisance. This will include psychological harm and distress, which falls outside the scope of private nuisance. It is the harm to the claimant's use or value of their land, caused by the visual intrusion of the defendant, which gives rise to the cause of action.

---

14 *Hunter v Canary Wharf Ltd* [1997] AC 655, 687G, 702G

15 *Fearn & Ors v Board of Trustees of the Tate Gallery* [2024] AC 1 (SC) at [9]-[11]

16 *Fearn & Ors v Board of Trustees of the Tate Gallery* [2024] AC 1 (SC) at [11]

17 *Hunter v Canary Wharf Ltd* [1997] AC 655, 724H

Parties to the action

The fundamental nature of private nuisance as a tort of land determines who can, and who cannot, bring a claim within the cause of action. As per Lord Goff in *Hunter*:

> *"An action in private nuisance will only lie at the suit of a person who has a right to the land affected. Ordinarily, such a person can only sue if he has the right to exclusive possession of the land, such as a freeholder or tenant in possession, or even a licensee with exclusive possession. Exceptionally…this category may include a person in actual possession who has no right to be there; and in any event a reversioner can sue in so far as his reversionary interest is affected. But a mere licensee on the land has no right to sue."* [18]

Generally speaking, it is therefore the party with exclusive possession of the affected property who has the right to sue for nuisance. A reversioner may have a right to bring a claim if the nuisance has caused damage to the reversion. This is ultimately a question of the permanence of that damage,[19] which has been defined as an act that will continue indefinitely unless something is done to remove it.[20] How this might relate to a visual intrusion case will of course depend on the particular nature of the interference in question. In *Fearn*, it was the invitation of several hundred thousands of visitors a year to use the platform that gave rise to liability, and not the construction of the viewing platform overlooking the claimants' land itself. It is unlikely that the invitation would be viewed as sufficiently permanent to have caused damage to the reversion. As such, the claimants'

---

18 *Hunter v Canary Wharf Ltd* [1997] AC 655, 692C

19 *Hunter v Canary Wharf Ltd* [1997] AC 655, 688E

20 *Jones v Llanrwst Urban DC (No.2)* [1911] 1 Ch. 393, 404

landlord would not have had standing to bring a claim. If the offending act of intrusion consisted of the erection of several CCTV cameras on the defendant's land (see Chapter Three), this might be considered a permanent state of affairs and therefore give the reversioner of the land being filmed standing to bring a claim.

In respect of the party to be sued, there is for present purposes no need to go beyond the summary of the law given by Lord Millett in *Southwark LBC v Mills*:

> *"Once the activities complained of have been found to constitute an actionable nuisance, more than one party may be held legally responsible. The person or persons directly responsible for the activities in question are liable; but so too is anyone who authorised them. Landlords have been held liable for nuisances committed by their tenants on this basis. It is not enough for them to be aware of the nuisance and take no steps to prevent it. They must either participate directly in the commission of the nuisance, or they must be taken to have authorised it by letting the property...but they cannot be held liable in tort for having authorised the commission of an actionable nuisance unless what they have authorised is an actionable nuisance."*[21]

Substantial interference with ordinary use of land

In order to be actionable as a nuisance, the act complained of must amount to a 'substantial interference with the ordinary use of land.' This principle will likely be the battleground for most cases involving visual intrusion (as it was in *Fearn*). The test to be applied, and in particular its relation to the principle of 'unreasonable user', was

21 *Southwark LBC v Mills* [2001] 1 AC, 21H

considered in detail in Lord Leggatt's lead judgment in the Supreme Court in *Fearn*. On the view taken by the dissenting minority (given voice in Lord Sales' judgment) the test which following *Fearn* is now law represents a departure from the previous position. The nature of this element of the tort, which requires consideration in greater detail, is discussed in Chapter Two.

Damage and foreseeability

The tort of private nuisance is actionable only on proof of damage, and is not actionable *per se* (as, for example, with trespass);[22] until damage is caused, no cause of action exists, only the potentiality of a nuisance.[23] However, as stressed by Sir Terrence Etherton MR in *Williams v Network Rail Infrastructure Ltd*,[24] this principle must be treated with caution. It is not necessary before liability for visual intrusion can be established that actual physical damage has been caused to the land. In relation to nuisance by interference with the use and enjoyment of land (which, as discussed above, visual intrusion is likely to constitute), the requirement of damage will be satisfied by establishing the undue interference itself;[25] the loss of the land's intangible amenity value is sufficient.[26]

---

22 *Jalla v Shell International Trading and Shipping Co Ltd* [2023] UKSC 16 at [3]

23 *Sedleigh Denfield v O'Callaghan* [1940] AC 880, 896

24 *Williams v Network Rail Infrastructure Ltd* [2019] QB 601 at [42]-[43]

25 *Jalla v Shell International Trading and Shipping Co Ltd* [2023] UKSC 16 at [3]

26 Terrence Etherton MR in *Williams v Network Rail Infrastructure Ltd* [2019] QB 601 at [42], and in *Fearn & Ors v Board of Trustees of the Tate Gallery* [2020] Ch. 621 (CA) at [34]

It is settled that foreseeability of harm is a pre-requisite for the recovery of damages for private nuisance.[27] Where a claim arising out of visual intrusion seeks damages, recovery will therefore be limited to compensation for the damage to the use of the land that was reasonably foreseeable. However, a question remains in respect of the relevance of foreseeability as an element of <u>liability</u> as opposed to simply the recovery of damages: does the damage (which as above is essential to the cause of action) need to be foreseeable in order to establish liability if, for example, only injunctive relief is sought?

In certain categories of nuisance, this has been settled in the affirmative, for example where liability in nuisance arises for failing to abate a hazard to neighbouring land (see the cases following *Goldman v Hargrave*[28] and *Leakey v National Trust*[29]) and cases on encroachment (*Delaware Mansions Ltd v Westminster City Council*[30]). However, in *The Wagon Mound (No.2),* Lord Reid expressly recognised that there are some cases of nuisance where foreseeability is not an element of liability.[31] It may be that Lord Reid was seeking to distinguish between private nuisance and public nuisance, in which liability is strict (ie foreseeability is not necessary); or, that he was seeking to distinguish cases in which fault plays a part in liability:

---

27 *Overseas Tankship (UK) Ltd v Miller Steamship (The Wagon Mound (No.2))* [1967] 1 AC 617, 640B; *Cambridge Water Co v Eastern Counties Leather* [1994] 2 AC 264, 301C-D

28 *Goldman v Hargrave* [1967] 1 AC 645

29 *Leakey v National Trust* [1980] QB 485

30 *Delaware Mansions Ltd v Westminster City Council* [2001] UKHL 55

31 *Overseas Tankship (UK) Ltd v Miller Steamship (The Wagon Mound (No.2))* [1967] 1 AC 617, 640

> *"Although negligence may not be necessary [to establish liability in nuisance], fault of some kind is almost always necessary and fault generally involves foreseeability."* [32]

The relevance of foreseeability as an element of liability was not raised in *Lawrence* or *Fearn*, (not at first instance, Court of Appeal nor Supreme Court level), both of which were cases concerning interference with use and amenity. This absence in itself may suggest that foreseeability is not a distinct element of liability in such cases. In *Fearn,* Lord Leggatt did have regard to the fact that the visual intrusion caused by the viewing gallery was foreseeable;[33] however, he sought to explain the finding of nuisance in the New Zealand interference case of *Bank of New Zealand v Greenwood*[34] on the basis that the interference caused '*was so unusual and unforeseeable as to be beyond anything that could actually be expected*'.[35] Nevertheless, the judgment of Lord Goff in *Cambridge Water Co. Eastern Counties Leather*[36] does suggest that foreseeability is an element of liability in interference with use cases:

> *"It is still the law that the fact that the defendant has taken all reasonable care will not of itself exonerate him from liability, the relevant control mechanism being found within the principle of reasonable user. But it by no means follows*

32 *Overseas Tankship (UK) Ltd v Miller Steamship (The Wagon Mound (No.2))* [1967] 1 AC 617, 639

33 *Fearn & Ors v Board of Trustees of the Tate Gallery* [2024] AC 1 (SC) at [49]

34 *Bank of New Zealand v Greenwood* [1984] 1 NZLR 525

35 *Fearn & Ors v Board of Trustees of the Tate Gallery* [2024] AC 1 (SC) at [77]

36 *Cambridge Water Co. Eastern Counties Leather* [1994] 2 AC 264

> *that the defendant should be held liable for damage of a type which he could not reasonably foresee…for if a plaintiff is in ordinary circumstances only able to claim damages in respect of personal injuries where he can prove such foreseeability on the part of the defendant, it is difficult to see why, in common justice, he should be in a stronger position to claim damages for interference with the enjoyment of his land where the defendant was unable to foresee such damage."*[37]

In the dissenting judgment in *Fearn*, following *Cambridge Water,* Lord Sales found the question of whether or not the interference is reasonably foreseeable to be a factor in the wider test of 'unreasonable user';[38] as discussed in Chapter Two, the majority disavowed such a test, which is now framed in terms of 'common and ordinary use'. It is therefore unclear whether foreseeability of damage is an element of liability (as opposed to recoverability of damages) for nuisance for interference with the use and enjoyment of land, and if it is, how it fits in with the test for liability arising out of Lord Leggatt's judgment in *Fearn*.

---

37 *Cambridge Water Co. Eastern Counties Leather* [1994] 2 AC 264, 300

38 *Fearn & Ors v Board of Trustees of the Tate Gallery* [2024] AC 1 (SC) at 167

CHAPTER TWO

ACTIONABLE INTERFERENCE AND 'UNREASONABLE USER' IN LIGHT OF *FEARN*

Not every interference with a person's use and enjoyment of their land will be an actionable nuisance. Various terms have been applied to describe an act that will give rise to liability, such as 'undue', 'unlawful' and, as given detailed consideration in the Supreme Court in *Fearn*, 'unreasonable'. However, as Lord Leggatt was at pains to emphasise, 'reasonableness' is not a test to be applied to determine liability.[1] Rather, Lord Leggatt has identified several principles which, whilst not '*formulae or mechanical rules*', are expressed as a framework of questions that the court should ask:[2]

(1) Firstly, whether the defendant's use of land has caused a <u>substantial interference</u> with the ordinary use of the <u>claimant's</u> land;

(2) Secondly, if so, whether in any event the activity is itself no more than an ordinary use of the <u>defendant's</u> own land, and whether that use is 'conveniently done'

---

1 *Fearn & Ors v Board of Trustees of the Tate Gallery* [2024] AC 1 (SC) at [80]

2 *Fearn & Ors v Board of Trustees of the Tate Gallery* [2024] AC 1 (SC) at [20]-[21]

The underlying justification for this approach is not the principle of reasonableness, or reasonable user. Rather, it is one of good neighbourliness and reciprocity.[3]

It is necessary to consider Lord Leggatt's judgment on this element of the cause of action in some detail. Whilst *Fearn* may well have some lasting impact as a gateway through which visual intrusion cases can enter the law of nuisance, its most consequential contribution will likely be Lord Leggatt's discussion of this issue. Every case of visual intrusion, as with all cases of nuisance for interference with use more generally, will need to be assessed against these principles to determine whether the offending act is actionable as a tort.

Further, it was on this issue that the two dissenting justices departed from the majority. As expressed in the judgment of Lord Sales, there is some argument that this constitutes a departure from the previous position. Given this has arisen in the context of visual intrusion, it is appropriate to discuss it here.

The Judgment of the Majority in *Fearn*

Regardless of the strength of the dissenting position (as held by Lord Sales and Lord Kitchen), or whether it departs from previous authority, the judgment of Lord Leggatt on this issue is now the law. It should be the starting point for all future consideration of the question of what amounts to a substantial interference. The judgment speaks for itself, and the following is only intended as a summary of the key principles:

---

3 *Fearn & Ors v Board of Trustees of the Tate Gallery* [2024] AC 1 (SC) at [34]

(1) An interference will not be substantial where it is trifling, small or minor, as it must '*sensibly diminish the comfort, enjoyment or value of the property which is affected*'[4] (as per Carnwath LJ in *Barr v Biffa Waste Services Ltd,* there is no absolute standard for this question, and it is a question of degree to be decided by reference to all of the circumstances of the case[5]).

(2) The test to be applied is objective, judged by the standards of what an ordinary or average person in the claimant's position would find annoying or inconvenient.[6]

(3) If the use of the claimant's land being interfered with is not an ordinary use of that land, then no actionable nuisance will arise.[7] This reflects the principle that '*a man cannot increase the liabilities of his neighbour by applying his own property to special uses*'.[8]

(4) Even where the defendant's activity substantially interferes with the ordinary use of the claimant's land, no liability will arise if the activity is no more than the ordinary use of the

---

4 *Fearn & Ors v Board of Trustees of the Tate Gallery* [2024] AC 1 (SC) at [22]

5 *Barr v Biffa Waste Services Ltd* [2013] QB 455 at [36(i)]

6 *Fearn & Ors v Board of Trustees of the Tate Gallery* [2024] AC 1 (SC) at [23]

7 *Fearn & Ors v Board of Trustees of the Tate Gallery* [2024] AC 1 (SC) at [25]

8 *Eastern and South African Telegraph Co Ltd v Cape Town Tramways Co Ltd* [1902] AC 381, 393

defendant's own land.[9] The test is as per the classic statement of Bramwell B in *Bamford v Turnley*:

> *"those acts necessary for the common and ordinary use and occupation of land and houses may be done, if conveniently done, without subjecting those who do them to an action"* [10]

The second of these conditions, namely that the act be '*conveniently done,*' will be satisfied where it is done with proper consideration for the interests of neighbouring occupiers.

(5) It is no answer to a claim for nuisance to say that the defendant is using its land reasonably; the test to be applied is that of the two conditions given by Bramwell B.[11]

(6) Following *Sturgess v Bridgman,* [12] the question of what constitutes the common and ordinary use of land is to be judged having regard to the character of the locality[13] (as per Lord Neuberger in *Lawrence v Fen Tigers Ltd,* an assessment of the character of the locality should take into account the

---

9 *Fearn & Ors v Board of Trustees of the Tate Gallery* [2024] AC 1 (SC) at [27]

10 *Bamford v Turnley* (1862) 3 B & S 66, 83

11 *Fearn & Ors v Board of Trustees of the Tate Gallery* [2024] AC 1 (SC) at [31]

12 *Sturgess v Bridgman* (1879) 11 Ch D 852

13 *Fearn & Ors v Board of Trustees of the Tate Gallery* [2024] AC 1 (SC) at [38]-[39]

defendant's activities, but leaving them out to the extent they are a nuisance[14]).

These principles and tests derive from and give effect to the underlying importance of reciprocity between neighbours, which is a rule of "give and take, live and let live". This principle, which is one of equal justice,[15] will apply wherever a nuisance results from the ordinary use of land.[16] Lord Leggatt provides a neat summary of the application of this principle:

> *"A person who puts his land to a special use cannot justify substantial interference which this causes with the ordinary use of neighbouring land by saying that he is asking no more consideration or forbearance from his neighbour than they (or an average person in their position) can expect from him. Nor can such a person complain on that basis about substantial interference with his special use of land caused by the ordinary use of neighbouring land. By contrast, a person who is using her land in a common and ordinary way is not seeking any unequal treatment or asking of her neighbours more than they ask of her."*[17]

Applying Lord Leggatt's test, a claimant will therefore succeed if he can show that: (1) the interference caused by the activity is substantial; (2) the ordinary use of his land is being interfered with; (3) the activity

---

14 *Lawrence v Fen Tigers Ltd* [2014] AC 822 [63]-[65]

15 *Fearn & Ors v Board of Trustees of the Tate Gallery* [2024] AC 1 (SC) at [34]

16 *Fearn & Ors v Board of Trustees of the Tate Gallery* [2024] AC 1 (SC) at [28]

17 *Fearn & Ors v Board of Trustees of the Tate Gallery* [2024] AC 1 (SC) at [35]

is outside the ordinary use of the defendant's land; or (4) if it is within the ordinary use of the defendant's land, it is not conveniently done.

The Locality Principle

As above, one of the principles highlighted by the Supreme Court in *Fearn* (which also received considerable attention in *Lawrence v Fen Tigers Ltd*[18]), is that the determination of what constitutes the common and ordinary use of land must have regard to the character of the locality of the land in question. This follows the famous expression of this principle in *Sturges v Bridgman*:[19]

> *whether anything is a nuisance or not is a question to be determined, not merely by an abstract consideration of the thing itself, but in reference to its circumstances; what would be a nuisance in Belgrave Square would not necessarily be so in Bermondsey; and where a locality is devoted to a particular trade or manufacture carried on by the traders or manufacturers in a particular and established manner not constituting a public nuisance, Judges and juries would be justified in finding, and may be trusted to find, that the trade or manufacture so carried on in that locality is not a private or actionable wrong.*

Thesiger LJ was not, as has sometimes been supposed, making disparaging comments about the locale of Bermondsey. Rather, the relevant point is that an activity about which a claimant could rightly complain in a solely residential area may, by virtue of an area's

18 *Lawrence v Fen Tigers Ltd* [2014] AC 22

19 *Sturges v Bridgman* (1879) 11 Ch D 852

industrial character, not amount to a nuisance: it is entirely context dependent.

Lord Neuberger, commenting generally on the locality principle in *Lawrence v Fen Tigers Ltd*, highlighted the difficulties in identifying the precise extent of the locality, or the precise words to describe its character. He noted that the concept of 'character' may be too monolithic, and instead suggested that 'the established pattern of uses' in the locality may afford judges more guidance.[20] Lord Carnwath echoed this difficulty, recognising that *'a locality may not conform to a single homogenous identity, but rather may consist of a varied pattern of uses all of which need to coexist in a modern society.'*[21] The precise issue in *Lawrence* was the extent to which the judge is entitled to take into account the defendant's use, of which complaint is made, in considering the nature of the character of the locality. Lord Neuberger held as follows:

> *"It seems clear that the character of the locality must be assessed by reference to the position as it is as a matter of fact, save to the extent that any departure from reality, or artificial assumption, should be made as a matter of logical or legal requirement (the presumption of reality). Accordingly, in a nuisance claim, I accept that one starts, as it were, with the proposition that the defendant's activities are to be taken into account when assessing the character of the locality."*[22]

This conclusion is echoed by Lord Carnwath, who considered that '*an existing activity can in my view clearly be taken into account if it is part*

---

20 *Lawrence v Fen Tigers Ltd* [2014] AC 22at [59]-[60]

21 *Lawrence v Fen Tigers Ltd* [2014] AC 22 at [181]

22 *Lawrence v Fen Tigers Ltd* [2014] AC 22 at [63]

of the established pattern of use.'[23] However, Lord Neuberger introduced an important qualification to this starting point:

> *"To the extent that those activities are a nuisance to the claimant, they should be left out of account when assessing the character of the locality, or, to put it another way, they should be notionally stripped out of the locality when assessing its character."*[24]

Lord Neuberger candidly accepted that there is an element of circularity to this approach, but that it is likely to be offset by the clarity, in most cases, once the facts have been established, of determining whether an act is a nuisance without having to answer precise questions of the character of the locality, and in any event it is preferable to the alternatives.[25]

Locality may well play a part in many of the factual scenarios in which visual intrusion might arise, as considered in the next Chapter. In particular, the nature of urban spaces in which people are necessarily forced to live in closer confines to each other is likely to inform the extent to which a potential act of visual intrusion can be considered to be outside the common and ordinary usage of land.

---

23 *Lawrence v Fen Tigers Ltd* [2014] AC 22 at [187]

24 *Lawrence v Fen Tigers Ltd* [2014] AC 22 at [65]

25 *Lawrence v Fen Tigers Ltd* [2014] AC 22 at [71]-[73]

The Dissenting Judgment in *Fearn*

The difference between the approaches of majority and the minority in *Fearn* was the extent to which the test to be applied in any case is one of reasonableness. The point of departure was the judgment of Lord Goff in *Cambridge Water Co v Eastern Counties Leather*:

> "*...liability has been kept under control by the principle of reasonable user–the principle of give and take as between neighbouring occupiers of land, under which 'those acts necessary for the common and ordinary use and occupation of land and houses may be done, if conveniently done, without subjecting those who do them to an action'* [citing *Bamford v Turnley*]. *If the user is reasonable, the defendant will not be liable for consequent harm to his neighbour's enjoyment of his land; but if the user is not reasonable, the defendant will be liable, even though he may have exercised reasonable care and skill to avoid it.*"[26]

In the view of the majority in *Fearn*, this was simply an endorsement of the principle espoused by Bramwell B in *Bamford v Turnley*, set out above, with the reference to reasonable user merely a shorthand for the principle of reciprocity. Lord Leggatt expressly disavowed any attempt to read into Lord Goff's judgment a suggestion that the applicable test is one of reasonableness.[27] This informed his criticism of the judge at first instance:

> "[The judge] *thought that an overall assessment was required of what – in an undefined sense – is "reasonable" in all the*

---

26 *Cambridge Water Co v Eastern Counties Leather* [1994] 2 AC 264, 299

27 *Fearn & Ors v Board of Trustees of the Tate Gallery* [2024] AC 1 (SC) at [29

> *circumstances. He treated the rule of give and take as if it were an element of such an assessment of "reasonableness" rather than a principle of reciprocity and equal justice. And he asked himself whether the nature of the Tate's use of land is "reasonable", instead of asking whether it is a common and ordinary use."* [28]

Lord Sales, dissenting, took the opposite view. He read Lord Goff's judgment as endorsing '*an objective reasonableness test informed by the basic principle of give and take*'.[29] Lord Sales argues forcefully and at some length both as to why this is the correct position arising from the authorities, and also why it is preferable to a test based on 'common and ordinary use' alone. To understand their dissenting Lordships' position and reasoning, the judgment of Lord Sales should be read in its entirety, but to summarise his argument in broad terms:

(1) *Bamford v Turnley* was a case emphasising the principle of reasonable reciprocity and compromise, as one had to look at and take into account the use and interests of both claimant and defendant. This principle, applied in *Southwark London Borough Council v Tanner*[30] and in *Biffa Waste*,[31] is why it is

28 *Fearn & Ors v Board of Trustees of the Tate Gallery* [2024] AC 1 (SC) at [54]

29 *Fearn & Ors v Board of Trustees of the Tate Gallery* [2024] AC 1 (SC) at [247]

30 *Southwark London Borough Council v Tanner* [2001] 1 AC 1

31 *Barr v Biffa Waste Services Ltd* [2013] QB 455

not a defence to say that use of the land complained of was reasonable.[32]

(2) This amounts to an objective principle of reasonable user. It is the application of this principle that renders the use by a defendant of land in a common and ordinary way, done conveniently, a defence to a claim in nuisance. Further, use of the defendant's land that is not common and ordinary does not necessarily constitute an actionable nuisance: an assessment of reasonableness, taking into account a range of factors, is required.[33]

(3) This principle cannot be reduced to the simple question of whether the defendant's use is common and ordinary; doing so places excessive weight on one side of the two-sided relationship, losing the essence of the principle of reciprocity. Further, doing so may frustrate the development of new uses of land which, whilst not 'common and ordinary,' are nevertheless objectively reasonable.[34]

(4) The test of objective reasonableness is both clear and workable (given that similar assessments are prevalent across the law of nuisance), and is better placed than a 'common and ordinary'

---

32 *Fearn & Ors v Board of Trustees of the Tate Gallery* [2024] AC 1 (SC) at [158-165]

33 *Fearn & Ors v Board of Trustees of the Tate Gallery* [2024] AC 1 (SC) at [166]-[167]

34 *Fearn & Ors v Board of Trustees of the Tate Gallery* [2024] AC 1 (SC) at [227]-[231]

> test to provide a solution across the whole range of cases falling within the categories of nuisance.[35]

It will be apparent that this approach is exactly what the majority identified as the incorrect legal test. It should be added that much of Lord Sales's criticism was directed at a test that considered the 'common and ordinary' use of the defendant's land only, without recourse to the use of the claimant's land. This, Lord Sales rightly maintained, departed significantly from the principles of reciprocity and "give and take" that have informed the law in this area. Lord Leggatt's test is not so narrow. As above, the first stage is to consider whether the claimant's use of land being interfered with is itself 'common and ordinary.'

It is beyond the scope of this work to assess whether or not Lord Sales was correct; rightly or wrongly, the law, and the test to be applied, is now derived from Lord Leggatt's judgment. Nevertheless, it is apparent from *Lawrence v Fen Tigers Ltd*[36] that, prior to *Fearn*, an objective assessment of reasonableness was a consideration in determining whether an interference was actionable. As per Lord Carnwath (echoing his judgment in *Biffa Waste*, and with whose conclusions Lord Neuberger expressly agreed[37]):

> *As I explained in [Biffa Waste], Lord Goff was not seeking to lay down a general rule, and the concept is not without its problems. The criterion of reasonableness has also been strongly criticised by some academics...In [Biffa Waste] I*

35 *Fearn & Ors v Board of Trustees of the Tate Gallery* [2024] AC 1 (SC) at [232]-[240]

36 *Lawrence v Fen Tigers Ltd* [2014] AC 822

37 *Lawrence v Fen Tigers Ltd* [2014] AC 822 at [5]

> *referred to Tony Weir's qualification of the reasonableness test:*
>
> *"Reasonableness is a relevant consideration here, but the question is neither what is reasonable in the eyes of the defendant or even the claimant (for one cannot by being unduly sensitive, constrain one's neighbour's freedoms), but what objectively a normal person would find it reasonable to have to put up with." (Weir, An Introduction to Tort Law, 2nd ed (2006), p 160.)*[38]

How, then, to treat this passage (and others in earlier authorities referring to reasonableness or a 'reasonableness test')? The answer may lie in Lord Leggatt's short section headed 'reciprocity'.[39] The tests to which he has given expression, traced to *Bamford v Turnley*, are distillations and expressions of the reciprocity principle. An overall consideration of objective reasonableness is not therefore the test, but it has informed the way in which the test is now to be framed. Some caution must be exercised in reading pre-*Fearn* authorities to ensure that references to reasonableness therein are understood in the context of Lord Leggatt's judgment.

---

38 *Lawrence v Fen Tigers Ltd* [2014] AC 822 at [179]

39 *Fearn & Ors v Board of Trustees of the Tate Gallery* [2024] AC 1 (SC) at [34]-[35

CHAPTER THREE

WHAT CONSTITUTES VISUAL INTRUSION?

The Complaint in *Fearn* and 'Overlooking'

It is necessary to isolate exactly what the basis of the complaint in *Fearn* was, to understand its use and limitation as authority for an act of visual intrusion. The unlawful action was not that the viewing platform overlooked the claimants' flats; nor was it that people in that building could look at and see inside the flats. These actions, classed as 'overlooking', are not actionable (see below).

Rather, the complaint in *Fearn* was as follows:

> *"What [the claimants] complain about is the particular use made by the Tate of the top floor. They complain that the Tate actively invites members of the public to visit and look out from that location in every direction, including at the claimants' flats situated only 30 odd metres away; that the Tate permits and invites this activity to continue without interruption for the best part of the day every day of the week; and that this has the predictable consequence that a very significant number of the roughly half a million people who visit the Tate's viewing gallery each year peer into the claimants' flats and take photographs of them."* [1]

---

1 *Fearn & Ors v Board of Trustees of the Tate Gallery* [2024] AC 1 (SC) at [92]

In other words, it was the invitation by the Tate of hundreds of thousands of visitors a year onto the viewing platform, and not the platform itself, nor the actual 'viewing' by those guests, that gave rise to liability. The rarity of the circumstances of *Fearn* will be immediately apparent. It is unlikely that factual circumstances directly analogous to this case will arise again. It is only conceivable that they might do so in respect of residential premises neighbouring comparable public spaces.

Where *Fearn* might be used to open the door for more common scenarios to emerge as private nuisances is in respect of acts which are based on, but go beyond, overlooking. Mere overlooking, by itself, will not give rise to liability. This is made expressly plain.[2] The term is given two definitions by Lord Leggat. The first is its 'conventional' usage, which refers to a spatial relationship:

> *"In ordinary speech the word refers to a spatial relationship between two places such that one affords a view, from a greater height, of the other – as in a statement such as "your flat overlooks my back garden".*[3]

This is not sufficient to give rise to liability in nuisance.[4] In reaching this conclusion, the Supreme Court followed several nineteenth-century authorities in which it was held that creating a new aperture in a wall of a property, and installing a window therein looking out onto a neighbour's property, would not give rise to an action in

2 *Fearn & Ors v Board of Trustees of the Tate Gallery* [2024] AC 1 (SC) at [89]

3 *Fearn & Ors v Board of Trustees of the Tate Gallery* [2024] AC 1 (SC) at [90]

4 *Fearn & Ors v Board of Trustees of the Tate Gallery* [2024] AC 1 (SC) at [90]

nuisance.[5] Further, the majority took into account the principle as affirmed in *Hunter v Canary Wharf Ltd* that, at common law, anyone may build whatever they like on their land, unless it violates an agreement not to do so or an easement.[6] Consequently, in *Fearn*, no complaint could be raised by the claimants about the construction of the viewing platform itself.

The second definition, termed by Lord Leggatt as 'unconventional', concerns the action of a person:

> *"The Court of Appeal in their judgment also use the term to mean looking at what is happening on land from a building which overlooks it"*[7]

Again, Lord Leggatt held that this would not by itself amount to a nuisance (emphasis added):

> *"In the ordinary course merely looking at what is happening on neighbouring land is not an actionable nuisance. It is hard to see how such an "act of overlooking" could by itself reasonably be regarded as anything more than a minor annoyance of a kind that neighbouring occupiers have to put up with under the rule of give and take, live and let live."*[8]

---

5 *Chandler v Thompson* (1811) 3 Camp 80; *Turner v Spooner* (1861) 30 LJ (Ch) 801; *Tapling v Jones* (1865) 20 CBNS 166

6 *Hunter v Canary Wharf Ltd* [1997] AC 655, 685D-F

7 *Fearn & Ors v Board of Trustees of the Tate Gallery* [2024] AC 1 (SC) at [91]

8 *Fearn & Ors v Board of Trustees of the Tate Gallery* [2024] AC 1 (SC) at [91]

As is clear from the highlighted wording, Lord Leggatt's judgment leaves open the possibility that such an act of overlooking could form the basis of a claim in nuisance, if it is outside the ordinary course, or constitutes something more than merely overlooking. It is likely that the future of this area of nuisance will largely be an exploration and a development of what factual circumstances go beyond mere overlooking sufficiently to give rise to liability.

Examples of Conduct that May give rise to Liability

Unusual examples in Fearn: Viewing Towers and Mirrors

Lord Leggatt does give some obiter consideration of what acts amounting to more than merely overlooking might give rise to liability. One example is a hypothetical situation in which a landowner erects a viewing tower, the only purpose of which is to enable views into the gardens and houses of other neighbours, and then charges an entry fee to allow members of the public to do so. This, he holds, would obviously substantially interfere with the ordinary use and enjoyment of the neighbour's land.[9] This, it will be apparent, is merely a parred down version of the facts of *Fearn*, with the invitation to view extended, perhaps, to tens of people, rather than hundreds of thousands. Much like the actual basis in *Fearn*, this hypothetical is unlikely to be a common occurrence.

What would the position be if, rather than paying members of the public, the only user of the viewing platform was the neighbour himself? Lord Leggatt referred to a medieval case from 1346 in which a fishmonger had admitted that building a watchtower looking onto a neighbour's land, with he and his family watching the neighbour

9 *Fearn & Ors v Board of Trustees of the Tate Gallery* [2024] AC 1 (SC) at [17]

daily, was a nuisance.[10] It is unlikely that this case, given its antiquity, can be treated as in any way authoritative, but it may strike the answer: whether or not this would constitute an actionable nuisance would depend on the extent of the intrusion, and in particular its frequency. If a defendant erected a tall tower in their garden, from which he occasionally surveyed his neighbour's property, it is unlikely that this would constitute an actionable nuisance; if he sat on that tower daily, using binoculars to see into his neighbour's home, or photographing and recording what he saw, this may well constitute visual intrusion.

Another example given in *Fearn*, again with a unique set of facts that is unlikely to re-occur, is the unreported case from 1904 involving the 'Balham dentist.' This case was referred to both by Lord Leggatt[11] and by Lord Sales, in respect of his finding that visual intrusion could amount to a nuisance (on which he agreed with the majority).[12] Lord Sales describes the case, quoting from a 1931 article by Professor Winfield entitled "Privacy"[13] as follows:

> *"A family in Balham, by placing in their garden an arrangement of large mirrors, were enabled to observe all that passed in the study and operating-room of a neighbouring*

10 *Fearn & Ors v Board of Trustees of the Tate Gallery* [2024] AC 1 (SC) at [16

11 *Fearn & Ors v Board of Trustees of the Tate Gallery* [2024] AC 1 (SC) at [103]

12 *Fearn & Ors v Board of Trustees of the Tate Gallery* [2024] AC 1 (SC) at [180]

13 (1931) 47 LQR 23

> *dentist, who sought in vain for legal protection against the annoyance and indignity to which he was thus subjected."*[14]

In echoing the opinion of Professor Winfield, both Lord Leggatt and Lord Sales suggest that these facts would likely give rise to a claim in nuisance for visual intrusion.

Observation, photography and CCTV

The introduction of filming or recording equipment may elevate an act of 'mere overlooking' into one of tortious visual intrusion. As Lord Leggatt notes, '*being photographed or filmed from neighbouring property is a far greater interference with the ordinary use and enjoyment of land than simply being observed with the naked eye.*'[15] This aligns with the outcome of several cases from other common law jurisdictions which were taken into account by Lord Leggatt in his assessment of whether or not visual intrusion was, conceptually, within the ambit of private nuisance.

One of these authorities was the New South Wales case of *Raciti v Hughes.*[16] In that case, as Lord Leggatt records, camera surveillance equipment had been aimed at the claimants' land, which was triggered by movement or noise on that land. In that case, the judge found that:

> *"On the evidence before me at the moment there is a deliberate attempt to snoop on the privacy of a neighbour and*

---

14 *Fearn & Ors v Board of Trustees of the Tate Gallery* [2024] AC 1 (SC) at [180]

15 *Fearn & Ors v Board of Trustees of the Tate Gallery* [2024] AC 1 (SC) at [103]

16 *Raciti v Hughes* (1995) 7 BPR 14837

> *to record that on video tape. It seems to me that this is an actionable nuisance...the facts of this case show that the surveillance and accompanying recording by video camera of what occurs in the plaintiffs' back yard gets sufficiently close to watching and besetting, and which...are an actionable nuisance."*[17]

It is notable that the judge justified his finding by analogy with the authorities on watching and besetting cases (see below). It may be that this was simply the door by which the judge chose to bring the offending action within the scope of nuisance, which can now be achieved by following *Fearn*. *Raciti* was followed by the New South Wales Supreme Court more recently in *Au v Berlach,*[18] which was not referred to in *Fearn*. In that case, the defendant installed seventeen CCTV cameras overlooking an accessway, some of which recorded constantly, some of which were motion-sensored, and some of which were triggered wirelessly. Content was uploaded onto the defendant's YouTube channel. The court agreed with the analysis in *Raciti*, finding that '*the use of the CCTV cameras is a substantial and unreasonable interference of [the claimants'] enjoyment of the Easement so that the cause of action in nuisance is made out.*'[19]

Another of the authorities cited is the Canadian case of *Suzuki v Munroe,*[20] in which the defendants had installed a surveillance camera overlooking the front yard, driveway and entrance of the claimants' home. The judge found that this constituted a nuisance:

---

17 *Raciti v Hughes* (1995) 7 BPR 14837, 14,840-14,841

18 *Au v Berlach* [2022] NSWSC 81

19 *Au v Berlach* [2022] NSWSC 81 at [117]

20 *Suzuki v Munroe* 2009 BCSC 1403

> *"I have no doubt that a surveillance camera continuously observing the entrance areas to a neighbouring property, or any part thereof, in these circumstances, is an intolerable interference with the use and enjoyment of the neighbouring property...no useful purpose of any kind is served by having the camera directed at any part of the Suzuki property. I am forced to conclude that the Munroes installed the camera and refused to remove or redirect it at least in part in order to provoke and annoy the Suzukis."* [21]

This passage raises a couple of relevant points. First, the absence of any legitimate purpose for the CCTV plainly operated on the judge's mind: in any visual intrusion case, this will likely factor into the consideration of whether or not the offending conduct is actionable. Second, the motivation of the defendants to provoke and annoy the claimants was a relevant factor. In *Hunter v Canary Wharf Ltd*, Lord Cooke, following *Christie v Davey*[22] and *Hollywood Silver Fox Farm Ltd v Emmett*[23] noting '*the versatility of human malevolence and ingenuity*,' suggested obiter that malice remained relevant in the assessment of nuisance.[24] This principle may well have a significant role to pay in the future development of nuisance by visual intrusion, especially where oppressive levels of surveillance, by CCTV or otherwise, are involved.

A similar point was considered, albeit briefly, in another British Columbian case, *Wasserman v Hall*.[25] In that case, the claimants

---

21 *Suzuki v Munroe* 2009 BCSC 1403 at [99]

22 *Christie v Davey* [1893] 1 Ch. 316

23 *Hollywood Silver Fox Farm Ltd v Emmett* [1936] 2 K.B. 468

24 *Hunter v Canary Wharf Ltd* [1997] AC 655, 721E

25 *Wasserman v Hall* 2009 BCSC 1318

sought to argue that their common law right to privacy had been infringed by the defendants photographing them in their back yard, aiming video surveillance cameras at their home, and attempting to see inside the windows from the defendants' property. This case was primarily concerned with breach of a statute applicable in that jurisdiction, but the court also found that:

> "*the tort of nuisance is sufficiently broad to encompass Mr Wasserman's video surveillance of the Hall residence as well…in my view, any owner of rural property would find it intolerable to have a tree-mounted video camera constantly aimed in the direction of his or her residence.*"[26]

The judge did not comment on the other complaints in the context of the tort of nuisance.

Reviewing these cases, Lord Leggatt distilled their common thread as being the presence of '*constant observation and photography*'.[27] It is likely that the same, in this jurisdiction, will give rise to liability in nuisance (provided the test is met), especially where it is done with the intention to annoy or intimidate a neighbour. Following *Fearn*, these will now be treated as cases of visual intrusion. The reference to the constancy of observation, and the consequent invitation to treat frequency as a relevant factor, aligns with an obiter observation in *Baron Bernstein of Leigh v Skyviews & General Ltd* in which the court found that the taking of a single photograph from an aeroplane above the claimant's property did not amount to a nuisance for the invasion of privacy:

---

[26] [85]-[86]

[27] *Fearn & Ors v Board of Trustees of the Tate Gallery* [2024] AC 1 (SC) at [102]

> *"Nor would I wish this judgment to be understood as deciding that in no circumstances could a successful action be brought against an aerial photographer to restrain his activities. The present action is not founded in nuisance for no court would regard the taking of a single photograph as an actionable nuisance. But if the circumstances were such that a plaintiff was subjected to the harassment of constant surveillance of his house from the air, accompanied by the photographing of his every activity, I am far from saying that the court would not regard such a monstrous invasion of his privacy as an actionable nuisance for which they would give relief."* [28]

In a 2021 reported County Court case, *Fairhurst v Woodard,*[29] Her Honour Judge Clarke dismissed a claim in nuisance caused by loss of privacy arising out of a video surveillance system and a "Ring" doorbell installed on the defendant's land that captured audio and video recordings of the claimant, his neighbour. The claim, which was brought under harassment, nuisance and under the Data Protection Act 2018, partially succeeded, but failed on the ground of nuisance. The judge's reasoning (which was correct at the time) was that, following the Court of Appeal decision in *Fearn*, she was prevented from making any finding of nuisance in this respect. She referred to the actions, following the Court of Appeal's lead, as "overlooking." It is possible that, following the Supreme Court's decision, and in line with the foreign authorities set out above, the claim in nuisance in *Fairhurst* may have succeeded on the facts of that case.

---

28 *Baron Bernstein of Leigh v Skyviews & General Ltd* [1978] QB 479, 489

29 *Fairhurst v Woodard* [2021] 10 WLUK 151

Loss of privacy

Several of the cases discussed above frame the tort as one of 'loss of privacy'. Invasion of privacy was the favoured term for the species of nuisance under consideration in the court of first instance in *Fearn*.[30] The availability of other causes of action outside of nuisance for the invasion of privacy featured heavily in the Court of Appeal's reasoning for not extending the tort to overlooking, with the court noting that it was '*invasion of privacy rather than...damage to property*' that was really the issue in cases of overlooking.[31] Use of the term 'loss of privacy' should, however, now be treated with some caution in respect of visual intrusion claims. Lord Leggatt in essence found that it was not a term of art:

> *"A further point is that "privacy" is a very broad term which encompasses an assortment of more specific concepts and human interests...the concepts of invasion of privacy and damage to interests in property are not mutually exclusive. An important aspect of the amenity value of real property is the freedom to conduct your life in your own home without being constantly watched and photographed by strangers...no new privacy laws are needed to deal with this complaint. The general principles of the common law of nuisance are personally adequate to do so."*[32]

30 *Fearn & Ors v Board of Trustees of the Tate Gallery* [2019] Ch. 369 (HC) at [133] *et seq*

31 *Fearn & Ors v Board of Trustees of the Tate Gallery* [2020] Ch. 621 (CA) at [84]

32 *Fearn & Ors v Board of Trustees of the Tate Gallery* [2024] AC 1 (SC) at [112]

It is therefore considered that, whilst loss of privacy may inform the nature of the interference with the use or amenity of land, it is not right to frame a case as one of nuisance by loss of privacy; following *Fearn*, the proper terminology and the species of nuisance should be 'visual intrusion', of which loss of privacy is merely a consequence.

Visual Intrusion Distinguished from Other Species of Nuisance

Finally, it is necessary to draw the line between visual intrusion and other species of nuisance which bear some similarity. The first of these are the 'watching and besetting' cases. In *J.Lyons & Sons v Wilkins* it was noted that:

> *"to watch or beset a man's house with a view to compel him to do or not to do what is lawful for him not to do or to do is wrongful and without lawful authority…such conduct seriously interferes with the ordinary comfort of human existence and ordinary enjoyment of the house beset, and such conduct would support an action on the case for a nuisance at common law."*[33]

In *Hubbard v Pitt* Lord Denning expressed a dissenting view that this had not stood the test of time, as watching and besetting, without more (such as obstruction or violence) would not amount to a nuisance;[34] nevertheless, the majority found that, in respect of the test for an interlocutory injunction, a prima facie case on this principle could arise.[35] These authorities informed Lord Sales's view in *Fearn* that nuisance was wide enough to cover instances of intense visual

---

33 *J.Lyons & Sons v Wilkins* [1899] 1 Ch. 255, 267

34 *Hubbard v Pitt* [1976] QB 142, 175G

35 *Hubbard v Pitt* [1976] QB 142, 189D

intrusion,[36] which as above was also the rationale in the Australian *Raciti* case. Nevertheless, whilst the acceptance (or arguable acceptance) of watching and besetting as a nuisance informed the development of visual intrusion as a species of the tort in itself, the two must be treated as distinct. *Fearn* cannot be read as an extension of the watching and besetting principle.

The second distinction, one expressly drawn by Lord Leggatt in *Fearn,*[37] is with the cases in which the claimant occupier is subjected, when looking out of their property, to a sight which is so offensive as to amount to a nuisance. Authority for this position is found in the Court of Appeal case of *Thompson-Schwab v Costaki,* in which the 'blatant perambulations' of prostitutes and their customers opposite the claimants' property was such as to '*force themselves upon the sight* [of the claimants]...*so as to constitute a sensible interference with the comfortable and convenient enjoyment of his residence*'.[38] This, and similar cases, are examples of tortious interference with the claimants' vision; they are not to be conflated with cases in respect of visual intrusion upon the claimant.

---

36 *Fearn & Ors v Board of Trustees of the Tate Gallery* [2024] AC 1 (SC) at [174]

37 *Fearn & Ors v Board of Trustees of the Tate Gallery* [2024] AC 1 (SC) at [16]

38 *Thompson-Schwab v Costaki* [1956] 1 WLR 335, 339

CHAPTER FOUR

DEFENCES TO VISUAL INTRUSION

The defences available in response to a claim of nuisance by visual intrusion are the same as those available in respect of any claim in nuisance, and it is beyond the scope of this work to consider them. Instead, the below examines several potential arguments that have been raised and discussed, particularly in the two more recent Supreme Court decisions of *Lawrence v Fen Tigers* and in *Fearn*, many of which have been found not to amount to defences. It is important to review these principles in order to understand the full extent of what will or will not amount to a tortious visual intrusion.

The Defendant's Right to Carry on an Activity

The defendant may have a right to carry on an activity which would otherwise be a nuisance. The claimant may have agreed to that activity being carried on, and therefore to the nuisance caused by it. Further, a claimant may otherwise be estopped from objecting to that activity.[1] In *Lawrence,* the Supreme Court considered the extent to which a right to create nuisance by way of noise could arise by prescription. The court found that the right to carry on an activity which results in noise, or the right to emit a noise, which would otherwise cause an actionable nuisance, is capable of being an easement, and therefore could arise by prescription.[2] The court also noted that, provided the

1 *Lawrence v Fen Tigers Ltd* [2014] AC 822 at [28]

2 *Lawrence v Fen Tigers Ltd* [2014] AC 822 at [33]

act is capable of being the subject of a valid grant, it could be too indeterminate to be an easement and still the right to carry it out could be acquired by prescription.[3]

Whether or not any particular act of visual intrusion is capable of being an easement, or indeed of being subject to a grant, will necessarily depend on the facts of each case. To take one example, it is unclear whether the right to film a property, by CCTV or otherwise, would fulfil this criteria. Rights to light and to air can be easements, but they concern the influx of either light or air to the property through a window or aperture. The right to emanate noise, or sound waves, or even smoke or smells from a property can also be an easement.[4] It is therefore possible that the right to receive light waves into a camera, or the right to film a certain view from a property, may be capable of being an easement. It is likely that the right to operate a camera is a right, in any event, capable of being granted, and will therefore be capable of arising by prescription irrespective of whether it can be an easement. The usual requirements of at least twenty years uninterrupted enjoyment as of right, being *nec vi, nec clam, nec precario* (not by force, nor stealth, nor with the licence of the owner)[5] will need to be satisfied. Defendants may have some difficulty in establishing the requisite frequency to satisfy the time period, as was discussed in respect of noise in *Lawrence*.[6]

If the defendant does not have such a right, it will not be an answer to a claim for nuisance to say that the defendant was using his land

---

3 *Lawrence v Fen Tigers Ltd* [2014] AC 822 at [32]

4 *Lawrence v Fen Tigers Ltd* [2014] AC 822 at [40]-[41]

5 *Lawrence v Fen Tigers Ltd* [2014] AC 822 at [31]

6 *Lawrence v Fen Tigers Ltd* [2014] AC 822 at [36]-[39]

reasonably.[7] This principle, which is of long standing, was reaffirmed in *Fearn*. If this were a defence, the principle of reciprocity underlying the tort would be out of balance, weighing heavily in favour of the defendant. Further, following *Fearn* and as discussed, a focus on 'reasonable' use is misleading. It is the extent to which both the claimant and the defendant's use is common and ordinary that will determine liability.

Coming to the Nuisance

It has long been held that it is not a defence to a claim in nuisance for the defendant to say that the claimant 'came to the nuisance', that is, that the act giving rise to what would otherwise be a nuisance was being carried out by the defendant before the claimant's use of the land commenced.[8] This principle was affirmed by both *Lawrence* and *Fearn*.

There are two limbs to this principle. First, it will be no defence to say that the defendant was already using his land in the manner complained of before the claimant acquired or began to occupy it, where the claimant is using his land in the same manner as it has always been used.[9] This is well settled. The second limb is that it will be no defence to say that the defendant's use of its land did not amount to a nuisance prior to the claimant changing the use of his land. In *Lawrence*, this came under scrutiny. Whilst Lord Neuberger

---

7 *Southwark London Borough Council v Tanner* [2001] 1 AC 1, 20; *Fearn & Ors v Board of Trustees of the Tate Gallery* [2024] AC 1 (SC) at [31]

8 *Sturges v Bridgman* (1879) 11 Ch. D. 852; *Miller v Jackson* [1977] 1 QB 966, 987

9 *Lawrence v Fen Tigers Ltd* [2014] AC 22 at [51]; *Fearn & Ors v Board of Trustees of the Tate Gallery* [2024] AC 1 (SC) at [42]

accepted that this was the case in respect of physical encroachment (following *Miller v Jackson*), and where the change in use was simply an extension to an existing building (as in *Sturges v Bridgman*), he expressed the following, obiter (agreed with, on this point, by Lord Carnwath):

> *"where a claimant builds on, or changes the use of, her land, I would suggest that it may well be wrong to hold that a defendant's pre-existing activity gives rise to a nuisance provided that (i) it can only be said to be a nuisance because it affects the senses of those on the claimant's land, (ii) it was not a nuisance before the building or change of use of the claimant's land, (iii) it is and has been, a reasonable and otherwise lawful use of the defendant's land, (iv) it is carried out in a reasonable way, and (v) it causes no greater nuisance than when the claimant first carried out the building or changed the use."* [10]

It is unclear whether Lord Neuberger's analysis would apply to a visual intrusion claim. First, this potential departure from the 'coming to the nuisance' principle has not been settled (the Supreme Court leaving it open in *Fearn*[11]). Second, visual intrusion claims are unlikely to arise from situations in which the senses of the claimant are affected, as they are for example in noise or smell cases. Nevertheless, as discussed in Chapter One, visual intrusion belongs to the same (informal) class of nuisance as noise and smell cases, and may well be analogous for the purposes of this point. It is conceivable that this issue might arise in a visual intrusion claim: if a defendant erected an extensive surveillance system on the boundary of his land, that land neighbouring an empty

---

10 *Lawrence v Fen Tigers Ltd* [2014] AC 22 at [56]

11 *Fearn & Ors v Board of Trustees of the Tate Gallery* [2024] AC 1 (SC) at [46]

field, and his neighbour then erected a dwelling close to the boundary and in the path of the defendant's cameras, this question would require an answer.

Sensitivity of the Claimant's Property

The walls of the *Fearn* claimants' flats at Neo Bankside which could be seen from the viewing gallery atop the Tate Modern were constructed with large floor to ceiling glass windows. There is no doubt that this design contributed to the level of intrusion and the level of interference with the use and amenity of those flats. As the judge at first instance noted, '*the architectural style in this case (including the more striking design of the block as a whole) has the consequence of an increased exposure to the outside world*'.[12] This led him to find that:

> "*the developers in building the flats, and the claimants as successors in title who chose to buy the flats, have created or submitted themselves to a sensitivity to privacy which is greater than would the case of a less glassed design. It would be wrong to allow this self-induced incentive to gaze, and to infringe privacy, and self-induced exposure to the outside world, to create a liability in nuisance.*" [13]

This, in essence, amounted to a finding that it would be a defence to a claim in nuisance that the claimants' property was unusually sensitive to the act complained of, such that any interference with use of the land was, at least in part, 'self-induced'. This approach has been

[12] *Fearn & Ors v Board of Trustees of the Tate Gallery* [2019] Ch. 369 (HC) at [206]

[13] *Fearn & Ors v Board of Trustees of the Tate Gallery* [2019] Ch. 369 (HC) at [205]

disapproved. The law, following the Supreme Court decision, is now as follows, and how sensitivity is to be approached is dependent on whether or not the defendant's use of their property is common and ordinary:

(1) If the defendant's use of their land is common and ordinary (taking into account factors such as the locality), then the sensitivity of the claimant's land to interference by that use is a relevant factor in determining liability. The example given by Lord Leggatt in *Fearn* was that, not of a public viewing gallery, but another block of flats built next to Neo Bankside. Occupants of that hypothetical building would have been able to see into the claimants' flats, causing annoyance. But provided this intrusion was simply in the ordinary course of the defendants' use of their land, it would not give rise to liability; in assessing the annoyance caused, the court could have regard to the design of the claimants' flats which, with floor to ceiling glass windows, were more sensitive than would otherwise be the case if they were constructed differently.[14]

(2) However, if the defendant's use of its land falls outside what is common and ordinary, it will not be a defence to say that the claimant's land is abnormally sensitive to visual intrusion caused by that use, or that the defendant's activity would not have caused the same level of annoyance if the claimant's building had been differently constructed or designed.[15]

---

14 *Fearn & Ors v Board of Trustees of the Tate Gallery* [2024] AC 1 (SC) at [62]-[64]

15 *Fearn & Ors v Board of Trustees of the Tate Gallery* [2024] AC 1 (SC) at [65]-[71]

Sensitivity of the claimant's building, then, is not a defence, but a factor that falls within the assessment of use as discussed in Chapter Two. However, the Supreme Court has left open the question of this issue at its extremity. Lord Leggatt recognised the possibility that '*there could be extreme cases where the design or construction of a building is so unusual and far from anything that could actually be expected*' that it might give rise to a defence to a claim in nuisance.[16]

Protective measures

It is not a good defence to a claim for visual intrusion to say that the claimant could take remedial steps to avoid the consequences of the defendant's acts. It offends the principle of reciprocity underlying the tort to place the burden on the claimant to mitigate the impact of an unusual use by the defendant of his property.[17] In *Fearn*, the measures rejected included lowering solar blinds, installing privacy films, installing net curtains, or screening the view with medium height plants.[18] In less rare settings, the same arguments will fail; if a neighbour erects excessive surveillance equipment on his property, he will not be able to argue that the claimant could mitigate the intrusion caused by shutting the curtains or otherwise screening the windows.

16 *Fearn & Ors v Board of Trustees of the Tate Gallery* [2024] AC 1 (SC) at [76]

17 *Fearn & Ors v Board of Trustees of the Tate Gallery* [2024] AC 1 (SC) at [83]-[84]

18 *Fearn & Ors v Board of Trustees of the Tate Gallery* [2019] Ch. 369 (HC) at [214]

Public Interest and Planning Permission

The Supreme Court in *Fearn*, following *Lawrence,* affirmed that it is wrong to treat questions of public interest as relevant to the question of liability for nuisance.[19] Its relevance lies in the question of remedy.[20] As per Lord Carnwath in *Lawrence*:

> *"I think there should be a strong presumption against allowing private rights to be overridden by administrative decisions [such as the grant of planning permission] without compensation. The public interest comes into play in the limited sense...in evaluating the pattern of uses "necessary...for the benefit of the inhabitants of the town and of the public at large", against which the acceptability of the defendant's activity is to be judged. Otherwise its relevance generally in my view should be in the context of remedies rather than liability."* [21]

Consequently, the fact that the continuance of an offending act, which would otherwise give rise to liability as a nuisance, may be in the public interest cannot be raised as a defence to a visual intrusion claim. Further, and related to that point, in assessing liability weight should not be given to the fact that planning permission has been granted for the activities that the claimant contends give rise to the nuisance:

> *"The mere fact that the activity which is said to give rise to the nuisance has the benefit of a planning permission is normally of no assistance to the defendant in a claim brought*

---

19 *Fearn & Ors v Board of Trustees of the Tate Gallery* [2024] AC 1 (SC) at [114], [120]

20 *Lawrence v Fen Tigers Ltd* [2014] AC 22 at [157]

Lawrence v Fen Tigers Ltd [2014] AC 22 at [222]

> *by a neighbour who contends that the activity cause[s] a nuisance to her land in the form of noise or other loss of amenity."*[22]

The justifications for this principle are given at length in the judgments of Lord Neuberger and Lord Carnwath in *Lawrence*, and it is not necessary to repeat them here. Planning permission may, nevertheless, have some relevance in the assessment of the nature of the locality. Lord Carnwath accepted that, in exceptional cases, policy decisions made by competent authorities may have led to '*a fundamental change in the pattern of uses, which cannot sensibly be ignored in assessing the character of the area against which the acceptability of the defendant's activity is to be judged.*[23] The role of the locality as relevant to an assessment of liability is discussed in Chapter Two.

It is conceivable that the decision in *Lawrence* in respect of public policy, and especially planning permission, will play into visual intrusion cases. There may well be public policy reasons as to why extensive surveillance systems, or the use of video-recording doorbells, should be permitted; these reasons could come into conflict with the private rights of those individuals whose properties are caught within the ambit of such surveillance. Further, to take Lord Leggatt's hypothetical example in *Fearn*, the viewing tower erected to which the paying public have access could have been erected with the benefit of planning permission. This would not prevent liability arising. Following *Lawrence*, where the act is otherwise a nuisance, it will be the private rights of the claimant which prevail.

---

22 *Lawrence v Fen Tigers Ltd* [2014] AC 22 at [93]

23 *Lawrence v Fen Tigers Ltd* [2014] AC 22 at [223]

CHAPTER FIVE

REMEDIES FOR VISUAL INTRUSION

One issue on which *Fearn* does not provide much by way of guidance is in respect of the remedy that might be granted for a visual intrusion claim. At first instance, having found that the conduct did not amount to a nuisance, Mann J declined to consider the question, save as to note that it was '*unlikely that I would have ordered any specific remedies.*'[1] He indicated that there might be alternatives to closing the gallery, but noted that this would have been for the Tate to raise.[2] In light of this, the Supreme Court determined that the question of remedy was not one which the court could decide, and remitted it to a further hearing in the Chancery Division.[3] This has not taken place. The principles that will be applicable to the grant of remedies for visual intrusion must therefore be found elsewhere.

1 *Fearn & Ors v Board of Trustees of the Tate Gallery* [2019] Ch. 369 (HC) at [223]

2 *Fearn & Ors v Board of Trustees of the Tate Gallery* [2019] Ch. 369 (HC) at [223]

3 *Fearn & Ors v Board of Trustees of the Tate Gallery* [2024] AC 1 (SC) at [131]-[132]

Injunctive Relief

The grant of an injunction

Where a claimant has succeeded in establishing that the defendant's activities constitute a nuisance, prima facie he will be entitled to an injunction to restrain the defendant from committing such nuisance in the future (in addition to damages for past nuisance, on which see below).[4] It should be noted that the *prima facie* right is for a prohibitory (negative) injunction, which prevents a party from doing an act. In contrast, a mandatory (positive) injunction, which compels a party to take some specific action, can never be granted "as of course"; every case must depend upon its own particular circumstances.[5] To illustrate the distinction by reference to one of the examples of visual intrusion discussed above, an injunction requiring the defendant to remove a complex surveillance system is mandatory; an injunction requiring the defendant to stop using a surveillance system in a manner that causes an interference to the claimant's land is prohibitory. It was the latter approach that was, in effect, taken by the court in British Columbia in the British Columbian CCTV case of *Suzuki v Munroe* referred to above.[6]

In *Redland Bricks v Morris,* Lord Upjohn laid down some principles for the application of the court's discretion to grant a mandatory injunction, (albeit qualifying that these are only in general terms):[7]

---

4 *Lawrence v Fen Tigers Ltd* [2014] AC 822 at [101]

5 *Redland Bricks v Morris* [1970] AC 652, 665

6 *Suzuki v Munroe* 2009 BCSC 1403 at [119]

7 *Redland Bricks v Morris* [1970] AC 652, *665-666*

(1) The claimant must show '*a very strong probability upon the fact that grave damage will accrue to him in future*'.

(2) The claimant must show that, if and to the extent such grave damage does occur, damages will not be a sufficient or adequate remedy (it should be noted that this principle followed *Shelfer v City of London Electric Lighting Co,*[8] and must, as discussed in more detail below, therefore be treated with some caution and read in light of *Lawrence*).

(3) The cost to the defendant to do works to prevent or lessen the likelihood of a future apprehended wrong must be taken into account. Where the defendant has acted '*wantonly and quite unreasonably in relation to his neighbour*' he may be ordered to carry out an act even if the expense is out of all proportion to the advantage given to the claimant, but where he has acted reasonably though wrongly, '*the cost of remedying by positive action his earlier activities is most important*'.

(4) If the court grants a mandatory injunction, it '*must be careful to see that the defendant knows exactly in fact what he has to do and this means not as a matter of law but as a matter of fact, so that in carrying out an order he can give his contractors the proper instructions.*'

In light of the judgment of the Supreme Court in respect of 'overlooking' (discussed above), and in particular the reaffirmation of the principle that a person may build whatever they please on their own land at common law (subject to the exceptions discussed), it is likely that injunctions in respect of visual intrusion claims will be prohibitory in nature. This will, of course, in every case depend on the particular interference complained of. To give the example of *Fearn*, as the Supreme Court found that the construction of the viewing

8 *Shelfer v City of London Electric Lighting Co* [1895] 1 Ch. 287

gallery itself was not a nuisance, Tate would not have been ordered to remove it. Rather, if an injunction had been granted (which was not in any event a guarantee) the court would likely have ordered Tate to stop inviting people onto the viewing platform in such numbers, which was the offending action. This would therefore have been prohibitory (of course, this discussion is necessarily speculative in the absence of any remedy having been granted, but is supported by the observation of Mann J at first instance that, had he granted an injunction, it would have been 'to restrain use' of the gallery[9]).

Damages in lieu of an injunction

The court may, pursuant to s.50 of the Senior Courts Act 1981, refuse to award an injunction and instead grant damages in lieu (a power which previously lay under the Chancery Amendment Act 1858, or Lord Cairns' Act as it was known; these are sometimes referred to in the authorities as Lord Cairns' Act damages). This principle may well have considerable relevance to visual intrusion claims (and appeared to be the direction in which Mann J's comments on remedy were pointing).

The court's jurisdiction to do so was considered extensively by the Supreme Court in *Lawrence v Fen Tigers Ltd.* Prior to *Lawrence*, the leading authority on the approach to be taken was the judgment of A L Smith LJ in *Shelfer v City of London Electric Lighting Co*:

> *"In my opinion, it may be stated as a good working rule that – (1) If the injury to the plaintiff's legal rights is small, (2) And is one which is capable of being estimated in money, (3) And is one which can be adequately compensated by a small*

9 *Fearn & Ors v Board of Trustees of the Tate Gallery* [2019] Ch. 369 (HC) at [222]

> *money payment, (4) And the case is one in which it would be oppressive to the defendant to grant an injunction: – then damages in substitution for an injunction may be given."* [10]

As Lord Neuberger noted, despite one line of authority recognising that the judgment in *Shelfer* had not intended to fetter the court's discretion, another has interpreted *Shelfer* strictly, to the effect that, unless all four conditions are satisfied, the court did not have jurisdiction to refuse the grant of an injunction.[11] The stricter interpretation has now definitively been disapproved. As per Lord Neuberger:

> *"It seems to me that (i) an almost mechanical application of A L Smith's four tests, and (ii) an approach which involves damages being awarded only in "very exceptional circumstances", are each simply wrong in principle…the court's power to award damages in lieu of an injunction involves a classic exercise of discretion, which should not, as a matter of principle, be fettered."* [12]

Lord Neuberger did identify some guidance to ensure that, whilst not fettered, the exercise of the discretion is done in a manner as predictable as possible:[13]

(1) The legal burden is on the defendant to show why an injunction should not be granted.

---

10 *Shelfer v City of London Electric Lighting Co* [1895] 1 Ch. 287, 323

11 *Lawrence v Fen Tigers Ltd* [2014] AC 22 at [110], [117]

12 *Lawrence v Fen Tigers Ltd* [2014] AC 22 at [119]-[120]; see also Lord Sumption at [161] and Lord Carnwath at [239]

13 *Lawrence v Fen Tigers Ltd* [2014] AC 22 at [121]-[123]

(2) Whilst each case turns on its facts, an injunction will be necessary to do justice and to serve as a warning to others where: the injury cannot fairly be compensated by money; the defendant has acted in a high-handed manner; the defendant has endeavoured to steal a march on the claimant or to evade the jurisdiction of the court.

(3) Again emphasising that each case turns on its facts, factors pointing against the grant of an injunction (without giving rise to any presumption or inclination) include whether there really is a question as to the legality of the obstruction and whether the defendant has acted fairly and not in an unneighbourly spirit.

(4) In the absence of additional relevant circumstances pointing the other way, it would normally be right to refuse an injunction if the four tests in *Shelfer* are satisfied. If those tests are not all satisfied, it does not mean that an injunction should be granted.

Criticising the *Shelfer* test, Lord Sumption added obiter his view that:

> "*an injunction should not usually be granted in a case where it is likely that conflicting interests are engaged other than the parties' interests. In particular, it may well be that an injunction should as a matter of principle not be granted in a case where a use of land to which objection is taken requires and has received planning permission.*" [14]

The law does not go this far, and other justices were at pains to stress that no such presumption should arise.[15] Lord Sumption also

---

14 *Lawrence v Fen Tigers Ltd* [2014] AC 22 at [161]

15 *Lawrence v Fen Tigers Ltd* [2014] AC 22 at [167], [246]

expressed a view that damages are ordinarily an adequate remedy for nuisance.[16] Lord Mance was critical of this position, noting that '*the right to enjoy one's home without disturbance is one which I would believe that many, indeed most, people value for reasons largely if not entirely independent of money.*'[17]

A final point arising from *Lawrence* is that public interest is a relevant factor in determining whether or not to grant an injunction or damages in lieu. The grant of planning permission for a particular activity may provide strong support for the contention that it is of public benefit, and therefore the existence of planning permission expressly or inherently authorising the activity which has caused the nuisance can be a factor in the determination (and one with real force).[18]

Measure of Damages in lieu

The starting point for the assessment of damages granted in lieu of an injunction will be the same as for damages for past nuisance (see below), but need not always be limited to the reduction in the value of the claimant's property; they might well also include the loss of the claimant's ability to enforce his rights, which may be assessed by reference to the benefit to the defendant of not suffering an injunction,[19] or the reasonable price for a licence to commit the nuisance.[20] This last point was expressly left open in *Lawrence* for

16 *Lawrence v Fen Tigers Ltd* [2014] AC 22 at [161]

17 *Lawrence v Fen Tigers Ltd* [2014] AC 22 at [168]

18 *Lawrence v Fen Tigers Ltd* [2014] AC 22 at [125], [157]

19 *Lawrence v Fen Tigers Ltd* [2014] AC 22 at [128]

20 *Lawrence v Fen Tigers Ltd* [2014] AC 22 at [173]

determination on a case by case basis, with caution expressed in respect of hypothetical negotiation damages where the injury to the property right, such as with interference with the enjoyment of land, is less specific.[21]

Damages

In addition to any injunctive relief, the claimant will be able to recover damages for the past commission of the nuisance. Nuisance is a tort, and the general tortious measure will apply, namely putting the claimant in the same position as he would have been if he had not sustained the wrong.[22] Further, nuisance is a tort to land, and it is the injury to the land that is the source of compensation. In respect of nuisance by interference with the enjoyment of land, as with other classes of nuisance, as held by the House of Lords in *Hunter v Canary Wharf Ltd,* the measure of damages is the diminution in the value of the land.[23] This will include both a diminution in the capital value of land, and also the amenity value.[24]

The diminution in capital value of land as a result of the presence of the nuisance will likely be assessed by reference to expert valuation evidence. In a case where an injunction has been awarded, the assessment will have reference to the factor that the defendant has been ordered to stop the offending conduct; nevertheless, this does not mean that an injunction eliminates diminution in capital value

---

21 *Lawrence v Fen Tigers Ltd* [2014] AC 22 at [248]

22 The classic statement of this principle is *Livingstone v Raywards Coal Co.* (1880) 5 App. Cas. 25, 39

23 *Hunter v Canary Wharf Ltd* [1997] AC 655, 696A-B, 724F-H

24 *Hunter v Canary Wharf Ltd* [1997] AC 655, 706D-F

entirely. As Patten LJ noted in *Raymond v Young*, a nuisance and harassment case:

> *"I do not therefore accept that the grant of a permanent injunction in the claimants' favour at trial is likely to be treated by a potential purchaser as a guarantee that they will not be subjected to the same treatment. The purchaser will know (or be advised) that the benefit of the injunction is personal to the Raymonds and that on a sale the protection it affords will effectively end. The Raymonds would cease on a sale to have any interest in continuing to enforce it and arguably have no locus to do so once they have parted with ownership of the Farm. Any further repetition of the same sort of conduct towards the incoming purchaser would necessitate fresh proceedings for an injunction with all the cost and trouble which that would involve."*[25]

Given there may well be overlap with harassment in a visual intrusion case (especially if it involves excessive use of surveillance equipment), this principle will likely be relevant.

Compensating the loss of amenity value of land has proven to be less straightforward. Following a review of *Hunter*, Patten LJ in *Raymond v Young* summarised the nature of the loss that the court is seeking to compensate:

> *"damages for what is commonly described as loss of amenity are damages for the diminution in the value of the right to occupy the affected property and not merely damages for the personal distress or inconvenience suffered by the individuals concerned. They are intended to and do compensate the claimant landowners for the distress and loss of amenity which*

25 *Raymond v Young* [2015] EWCA Civ 456 at [34]

> *they experience as a result of the nuisance but only in terms of the consequent loss in the use value of their property."* [26]

As the court in *Hunter* noted, the court may be dealing with intangibles,[27] and is being asked to quantify an injury that cannot necessarily be assessed mathematically.[28] The Court of Appeal in *Dobson v Thames Water Utilities Ltd* expanded on the approach to be taken in answering the question of how to assess damages where the only loss is loss of amenity:

> *"If the house in question was available to be let during the period of the nuisance, it may be that there would be direct market evidence of loss of rental value. Otherwise, it is perhaps inevitable that the assessment of damages for loss of amenity will involve a considerable degree of imprecision. But if estate agents are to assist in placing a value on the relevant intangibles, whether by calculating the reduction in letting value of the property for the period of the nuisance or in some other way, we would expect them in practice to take into account, for the purposes of their assessment, the actual experience of the persons in occupation of the property during the relevant period. It is difficult if not impossible to see any other way of proceeding."* [29]

This approach was followed by the High Court in the same case following remission for the assessment of damages. Ramsey J, with the assistance of valuation evidence, applied the diminution in the

---

[26] *Raymond v Young* [2015] EWCA Civ 456 at [27]

[27] *Hunter v Canary Wharf Ltd* [1997] AC 655, 706E

[28] *Hunter v Canary Wharf Ltd* [1997] AC 655, 696D

[29] *Dobson v Thames Water Utilities Ltd* [2009] EWCA Civ 28 at [32]-[33]

monthly rental value of the property for the period of the nuisance as a result of its presence as a '*sound basis on which to assess damages for loss of amenity,*' but noting that it would generally be a small percentage.[30] This approach was followed in the first instance decision in *Lawrence v Fen Tigers Ltd*.[31]

A claimant will also be able to recover other consequential losses.[32] In Ramsey J's decision in *Dobson v Thames Water Utilities Ltd*, which was a claim for nuisance by interference with use of land arising from noxious smells (and is therefore closer in comparison to visual intrusion than other forms of nuisance), the cost of items used in an attempt to overcome the nuisance were found to be recoverable.[33] If a claimant has incurred expense in trying to avoid nuisance caused by visual intrusion, for example by erecting blinds or screening, these costs will likely also be recoverable. However, as discussed above, following *Cambridge Water Co Ltd v Eastern Counties Leather*, in order to be recoverable, damages must be foreseeable.[34]

---

30 *Dobson v Thames Water Utilities Ltd* [2011] EWHC 3253 (TCC) at [1030]

31 *Lawrence v Fen Tigers Ltd* [2011] EWHC 360 (QB) at [313]-[323]

32 *Hunter v Canary Wharf Ltd* [1997] AC 655, 706F-H

33 *Dobson v Thames Water Utilities Ltd* [2011] EWHC 3253 (TCC) at [1016]

34 *Cambridge Water Co Ltd v Eastern Counties Leather* [1994] 2 AC 264, 301C-D

Limitation

Lastly, a word on limitation, which will depend on the remedy being sought by the claimant. If and to the extent the claimant is seeking injunctive relief, section 36 of the Limitation Act 1980 will have effect to disapply any limitation period. The equitable principles of acquiescence, delay and laches will nevertheless apply, and may well prevent the enforcement of any claim relating to an intrusion where action is not taken in an appropriate time. Delay will also inform the court's assessment of the need for any injunction.

Where the claim is for damages, section 2 of the Limitation Act 1980 imposes a limitation period of six years from the date on which the cause of action accrued (that is, in respect of nuisance, from the date on which actual damage was incurred: see the discussion in Chapter One of the nature of this damage). In light of the conclusion that mere overlooking does not constitute a nuisance, and the likely requirement of frequency or quantity to render any act of visual intrusion tortious, it is probable that most cases of visual intrusion will be ones of continuing nuisances. The Supreme Court in *Jalla v Shell International Trading* defined a continuing nuisance as follows:

> *"One where, outside the claimant's land and usually on the defendant's land, there is repeated activity by the defendant or an ongoing state of affairs for which the defendant is responsible which causes continuing undue interference with the use and enjoyment of the claimant's land. For a continuing nuisance, the interference may be similar on each occasion but the important point is that it is continuing day after day or on another regular basis…the cause of action therefore accrues afresh on a continuing basis."* [35]

---

[35] *Jalla v Shell International Trading* [2023] 2 WLR 1085 at [26]

Damages at common law for a continuing nuisance cannot be recovered for causes of action (ie for past occurrences of the continuing nuisance) that accrued more than six years before the claim was commenced.[36]

[36] *Jalla v Shell International Trading* [2023] 2 WLR 1085 at [32]

CONCLUSION

The Supreme Court's judgment in *Fearn& Ors v Board of Trustees of the Tate Gallery*[1] has potentially opened up a new frontier in nuisance. The facts of that particular case, which involved hundreds of thousands of visitors being invited onto the viewing gallery of the Tate Modern, are unlikely to be replicated. Nevertheless, in recognising that 'visual intrusion' is capable of amounting to a nuisance, the judgment in *Fearn* will have opened the door for new types of claims to succeed.

The question, which will be the focus of the development of the law in this area, is what falls within the scope of 'visual intrusion.' As with nuisance itself, the term will likely remain protean and without strict definition. As Lord Leggatt held, mere overlooking, without more, will not constitute a nuisance. Where the boundary lies between mere overlooking, and acts that are outside the ordinary course of overlooking, is open to be tested by future litigants. This work has provided some discussion of what might fall within the term; ultimately, this will only be decided by the nature of the claims that are brought.

The court in *Fearn* did not address the question of remedies. In this sense, future claims for nuisance based on visual intrusion will be entering new territory, and the applicable principles from other areas of nuisance will have to be relied on.

Lord Leggatt's judgment, arising in the context of visual intrusion, has clarified (or, from the position of the minority, rewritten) the law on the test for what will constitute an actionable interference. As

1 *Fearn & Ors v Board of Trustees of the Tate Gallery* [2024] AC 1 (SC)

discussed in Chapter Two, the test is that of the common and ordinary use of both the claimant and the defendant's land, having regard to the nature of the locality. This is founded on the principle of reciprocity, or good neighbourliness. As Lord Leggatt held, the test is not one of reasonableness and reasonable user. Alongside opening the door for nuisance claims under the heading of visual intrusion, Lord Leggatt's discussion of this case will likely prove to be the lasting legacy of the *Fearn* proceedings.

MORE BOOKS BY LAW BRIEF PUBLISHING

A selection of our other titles available now:-

'A Practical Guide to Confiscation and Restraint' by Narita Bahra QC, John Carl Townsend, David Winch
'A Practical Guide to the Law of Forests in Scotland' by Philip Buchan
'A Practical Guide to Health and Medical Cases in Immigration Law' by Rebecca Chapman & Miranda Butler
'A Practical Guide to Bad Character Evidence for Criminal Practitioners by Aparna Rao
'A Practical Guide to Extradition Law post-Brexit' by Myles Grandison et al
'A Practical Guide to Hoarding and Mental Health for Housing Lawyers' by Rachel Coyle
'A Practical Guide to Psychiatric Claims in Personal Injury – 2nd Edition' by Liam Ryan
'Stephens on Contractual Indemnities' by Richard Stephens
'A Practical Guide to the EU Succession Regulation' by Richard Frimston
'A Practical Guide to Solicitor and Client Costs – 2nd Edition' by Robin Dunne
'Constructive Dismissal – Practice Pointers and Principles' by Benjimin Burgher
'A Practical Guide to Religion and Belief Discrimination Claims in the Workplace' by Kashif Ali
'A Practical Guide to the Law of Medical Treatment Decisions' by Ben Troke
'Fundamental Dishonesty and QOCS in Personal Injury Proceedings: Law and Practice' by Jake Rowley
'A Practical Guide to the Law in Relation to School Exclusions' by Charlotte Hadfield & Alice de Coverley
'A Practical Guide to Divorce for the Silver Separators' by Karin Walker
'The Right to be Forgotten – The Law and Practical Issues' by Melissa Stock
'A Practical Guide to Planning Law and Rights of Way in National Parks, the Broads and AONBs' by James Maurici QC, James Neill et al
'A Practical Guide to Election Law' by Tom Tabori
'A Practical Guide to the Law in Relation to Surrogacy' by Andrew Powell
'A Practical Guide to Claims Arising from Fatal Accidents – 2nd Edition' by James Patience
'A Practical Guide to the Ownership of Employee Inventions – From Entitlement to Compensation' by James Tumbridge & Ashley Roughton
'A Practical Guide to Asbestos Claims' by Jonathan Owen & Gareth McAloon

'A Practical Guide to Stamp Duty Land Tax in England and Northern Ireland' by Suzanne O'Hara
'A Practical Guide to the Law of Farming Partnerships' by Philip Whitcomb
'Covid-19, Homeworking and the Law – The Essential Guide to Employment and GDPR Issues' by Forbes Solicitors
'Covid-19 and Criminal Law – The Essential Guide' by Ramya Nagesh
'Covid-19 and Family Law in England and Wales – The Essential Guide' by Safda Mahmood
'A Practical Guide to the Law of Unlawful Eviction and Harassment – 2nd Edition' by Stephanie Lovegrove
'Covid-19, Brexit and the Law of Commercial Leases – The Essential Guide' by Mark Shelton
'A Practical Guide to Costs in Personal Injury Claims – 2nd Edition' by Matthew Hoe
'A Practical Guide to the General Data Protection Regulation (GDPR) – 2nd Edition' by Keith Markham
'Ellis on Credit Hire – Sixth Edition' by Aidan Ellis & Tim Kevan
'A Practical Guide to Working with Litigants in Person and McKenzie Friends in Family Cases' by Stuart Barlow
'Protecting Unregistered Brands: A Practical Guide to the Law of Passing Off' by Lorna Brazell
'A Practical Guide to Secondary Liability and Joint Enterprise Post-Jogee' by Joanne Cecil & James Mehigan
'A Practical Guide to the Pre-Action RTA Claims Protocol for Personal Injury Lawyers' by Antonia Ford
'A Practical Guide to Neighbour Disputes and the Law' by Alexander Walsh
'A Practical Guide to Forfeiture of Leases' by Mark Shelton
'A Practical Guide to Coercive Control for Legal Practitioners and Victims' by Rachel Horman
'A Practical Guide to the Law of Driverless Cars – Second Edition' by Alex Glassbrook, Emma Northey & Scarlett Milligan
'A Practical Guide to TOLATA Claims' by Greg Williams
'A Practical Guide to Elderly Law – 2nd Edition' by Justin Patten
'A Practical Guide to Responding to Housing Disrepair and Unfitness Claims' by Iain Wightwick

'A Practical Guide to the Law of Bullying and Harassment in the Workplace' by Philip Hyland
'How to Be a Freelance Solicitor: A Practical Guide to the SRA-Regulated Freelance Solicitor Model' by Paul Bennett
'A Practical Guide to Prison Injury Claims' by Malcolm Johnson
'A Practical Guide to the Small Claims Track – 2nd Edition' by Dominic Bright
'A Practical Guide to Advising Clients at the Police Station' by Colin Stephen McKeown-Beaumont
'A Practical Guide to Antisocial Behaviour Injunctions' by Iain Wightwick
'Practical Mediation: A Guide for Mediators, Advocates, Advisers, Lawyers, and Students in Civil, Commercial, Business, Property, Workplace, and Employment Cases' by Jonathan Dingle with John Sephton
'The Mini-Pupillage Workbook' by David Boyle
'A Practical Guide to Crofting Law' by Brian Inkster
'A Practical Guide to the Law of Domain Names and Cybersquatting' by Andrew Clemson
'A Practical Guide to the Law of Gender Pay Gap Reporting' by Harini Iyengar
'NHS Whistleblowing and the Law' by Joseph England
'Employment Law and the Gig Economy' by Nigel Mackay & Annie Powell
'A Practical Guide to Noise Induced Hearing Loss (NIHL) Claims' by Andrew Mckie, Ian Skeate, Gareth McAloon
'An Introduction to Beauty Negligence Claims – A Practical Guide for the Personal Injury Practitioner' by Greg Almond
'Intercompany Agreements for Transfer Pricing Compliance' by Paul Sutton
'Zen and the Art of Mediation' by Martin Plowman
'A Practical Guide to the SRA Principles, Individual and Law Firm Codes of Conduct 2019 – What Every Law Firm Needs to Know' by Paul Bennett
'A Practical Guide to Adoption for Family Lawyers' by Graham Pegg
'A Practical Guide to Industrial Disease Claims' by Andrew Mckie & Ian Skeate
'A Practical Guide to Conducting a Sheriff Court Proof' by Andrew Stevenson
'A Practical Guide to Vicarious Liability' by Mariel Irvine
'A Practical Guide to Applications for Landlord's Consent and Variation of Leases' by Mark Shelton
'A Practical Guide to Relief from Sanctions Post-Mitchell and Denton' by Peter Causton

www.ingramcontent.com/pod-product-compliance
Lightning Source LLC
LaVergne TN
LVHW022311200926
848481LV00004B/1286
9781916698369